backstreet
boys

on the **road**
by Rob McGibbon

B⊞XTREE

First published 1999 by Boxtree an imprint of Macmillan Publishers Ltd
25 Eccleston Place London SW1W 9NF and Basingstoke

Associated companies throughout the world

ISBN 0 7522 1357 1

Text copyright © 1998 Rob McGibbon

9 8 7 6 5 4 3 2 1

A CIP catalogue record for this book is available from the British Library.

Designed by Blackjacks

Printed and bound in Italy by New Interlitho

PICTURE CREDITS

All Action/Todd Kaplan: 14–15; All Action/Phil Ramey: 39 (bottom); All Action/Reporters: 58–9; All Action/Paul Smith: 30–1; All Action/Starfile: 13 (centre); All Action/Justin Thomas: 34–5, 53.

Capital/Phil Loftus: 11; Capital/James McCauley: 6–7; Capital/Helene Wiesenhaan: 60.

Famous/Hubert Boesl: 10 (left), 12 (bottom), 16, 17, 18, 19, 32, 33 (bottom), 36–7; Famous/Fred Duval: 12 (centre top), 40–1, 52 (centre), 56; Famous/Rob Howard: 39 (top); Famous/Wilberto: 8, 9; Famous/Ian Yates: 52 (top).

Redferns/Paul Bergen: 2–3, 20–1, 22, 23, 24, 25, 26, 27, 28–9, 57; Redferns/Grant Davis: 12 (left & right top), 28 (left & right top), 33 (top), 35 (top), 38 (bottom), 42 (bottom), 44–5, 46–7, 48, 49, 50–1; Redferns/J M International: 10 (top), 13, 59 (bottom); Redferns/Michael Linssen: 38–9; Redferns: 43; Redferns/Simon Ritter: front cover, 1, 4, 42 (top), 47 (bottom), 52 (bottom), 54–5.

Contents

The incredible Backstreet Boys story began as far back as 1989, when an American millionaire called Lou Pearlman had the idea of creating a pop group in the mould of the 1980s teen phenomenon New Kids on the Block. Lou, a Florida-based entrepreneur, had made his fortune from an assortment of businesses after a failed career as a musician. Despite his enormous wealth, his heart still lay in music, so he decided to track down the best young talent he could find in his hometown of Orlando and turn them into superstars.

Thanks to Disney World, Sea World and the movie theme parks, Orlando is an international holiday destination and one of the entertainment centres of the east coast of America. The sprawling city is brimming with ambitious teenagers longing for a break in showbusiness and provided the perfect hunting

Introd

ground to find the talent Lou needed. As the New Kids faded in the early 1990s, he began his search by placing adverts in various Orlando newspapers and distributing flyers to drama schools, appealing for young guys who could sing and dance. Lou was rapidly inundated with hundreds of replies and the auditions began in June 1992 at his mansion.

The first boy chosen was Alexander James McLean, a charismatic fourteen-year-old with fantastic dance skills and a wacky personality that was perfect for the mad world of pop music. Next came Howie Dorough, a quieter lad compared to AJ, but with years of acting and singing experience. The third Florida boy selected was Nick Carter, a sweet-looking blond twelve-year-old with precocious star quality and a great voice.

Two other local lads were chosen for the early line-up of the group, but had to be replaced, which led to the discovery of Kevin Richardson. Kevin was working as a costume character at Universal Studios, while trying to build a new life away from his hometown of Irvine, in deepest Kentucky. He was spotted by a friend of Lou's and asked to audition. By a twist of fate, Kevin provided the final piece of the Backstreet puzzle when he introduced his cousin Brian Littrell to the group. Brian was a choirboy with an angelic voice who was still at school in Kentucky, but once Lou and the boys heard his voice, everyone knew his destiny lay with them in Florida.

The new line-up began singing together in April 1993 as the Backstreet Boys, taking the name from a now defunct flea market in Orlando. The boys trained hard to perfect their dance routines and the *a cappella* harmonising that would become their trademark. But it was not an easy ride to the top. For two years they travelled America, building up a fan base and trying to secure a record deal. There were countless rejections along the way until finally one record company took a gamble and released the Backstreets' début single 'We've Got It Goin' On' in August 1995. It bombed embarrassingly in America, but became a hit in Germany where boy bands were popular, so the Backstreet Boys concentrated their efforts in Europe.

Their success built steadily and throughout 1996 they recorded a string of hits including 'Get Down', 'I'll Never Break Your Heart' and 'Quit Playing Games (With My Heart)'. The buzz about the boys spread to Britain, the Far East, South East Asia and Canada, although they were still ignored in their home country. The pop star dream had come true and the boys' lives were a constant whirl of globetrotting and performing for thousands of adoring fans. By the beginning of 1997, the Backstreet Boys had sold millions of CDs and had become international celebrities, but they were not satisfied. When the group started, they had set themselves the ambitious target of becoming the biggest pop group in America since the New Kids on the Block. What follows is the story of how the Backstreet Boys finally made that dream come true.

uction

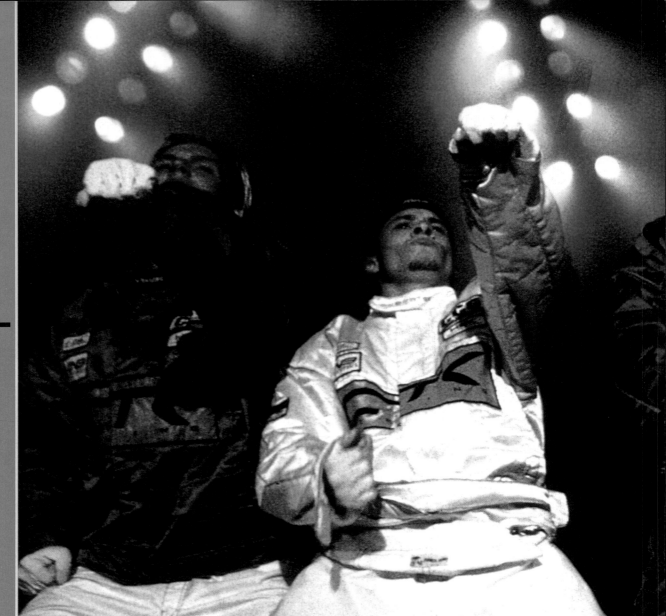

backst

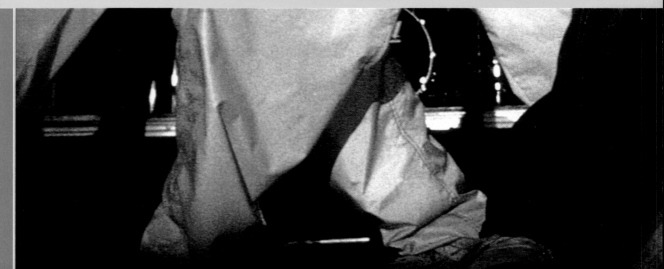

reet's
back

n June 1997, the Backstreet Boys headed home for America after finishing the British leg of their first major European tour. They arrived back in Orlando high on their success, which had seen their début album go gold and platinum in more than thirty countries and spawn a series of number ones and Top Ten hits. Anyone would have expected them to head straight for the beaches of Florida to reflect on their rise to pop stardom and relax in the knowledge that, after four long years of work, so many of their dreams had come true. The reality could not have been further from the truth.

Over the previous few months, Kevin, AJ, Howie, Brian and Nick had stolen time while touring to record some new songs for their second album. They already had a blend of soulful ballads and tuneful dance tracks worked out, but there was one great song which stood out above them all – 'Everybody (Backstreet's Back)'. It had a thumping dance rhythm and was a natural choice for the title track of the album. All it needed was a stunning video to match, so within days of returning to Orlando, the boys flew to Los Angeles to work on an extravagant mini-film that would ultimately help elevate them to the peaks of the pop world. On arriving in LA, they didn't head for the glamour of Hollywood and Beverly Hills, but opted instead for a giant disused aircraft hangar in a far-from-glitzy area on the outskirts of the city. To any onlooker, this was a nondescript building of no interest, but to the Backstreet Boys and a highly talented team of film-makers, it was the perfect venue to create what would become

the award-winning, smash hit video for 'Everybody'.

The idea for the promo had been dreamt up by the boys while touring, some eight months earlier. Back then, it had been a distant dream to make such an expensive video, as their modest success so far hardly warranted big budget ventures. But a lot had changed and now they were a world priority group in the eyes of their record company; the time had arrived for the boys to turn those wacky ideas into reality. The Backstreet Boys had set their hearts on a grand scale story set in a haunted castle, the centrepiece of which involved the boys turning into grisly ghouls of the night. The theme was a throwback to Michael Jackson's epic promo for 'Thriller', which had broken new ground for pop videos fourteen years earlier. Now the boys wanted to do it Backstreet-style for the 1990s.

As the sun blistered the LA tarmac outside, director Joseph Kahn began transforming the cavernous hangar into a series of sets that would represent different rooms in the eerie castle. Kahn, who is in his twenties, was relatively young to be behind the camera for such a big budget video, but he was ideal for the job. Because of his age, he got on well with the boys, and his imaginative modern-day twist on all things horror meant he was able to turn their raw ideas into a slick and stylised video that fitted the Backstreet Boys' young image. A vast amount of preparation had gone into the video. Sets had been designed and intricate prosthetics had been created to turn the boys into menacing monsters. There was also a large team of models and dancers on set to perform in a

number of sequences, particularly the closing ballroom spectacular which had been choreographed by the Backstreet Boys' expert dance coach, Fatima Robinson. The scale of the project meant that they faced all the usual frustrating problems associated with the making of a short movie, but without the luxury of time. The video had to be wrapped in just three days, so there was considerable pressure on the whole crew to get it right, especially Joseph Kahn and the stars of the show.

As the crew and designers assembled the sets in the hangar, each Backstreet Boy had his face slowly reconstructed by a team of make-up artists. The boys' patience was tested to the limit as they took it in turns to sit still for several hours while their hair, features and even their fingernails were painstakingly transformed. But the results proved to be worth every boring minute as, bit by bit, the faces that are adored by millions of fans were changed into far less attractive sights. Brian became the werewolf with wild hair, lethal fangs and a pimp-style fur coat; Nick unravelled into the

bulbous-nosed Mummy with rotting teeth; Howie's dark complexion made him perfect as a long-haired Count Dracula; Kevin was Dr Jekyll and Mr Hyde, the evil scientist with a split personality and disfigured face to match; and AJ became the hideously scarred Phantom of the Opera. Once the make-overs were complete, the boys took their places in the freshly prepared sets and Kahn's skilled direction turned them into wickedly cool pop stars in the house of horror. On the final day of the shoot, the set designers worked overtime to build a magnificent ballroom, where the boys and a host of dancers performed the big closing routine. Finally, after three days of solid work, it was a wrap, and Kahn locked himself away in the editing suite to fine-tune the footage and add the special effects.

Such was the weight of the Backstreet Boys' forthcoming schedule that they stayed in LA to film two more videos back-to-back for

future releases: 'As Long As You Love Me' and 'All I Have To Give'. These videos were less extravagant than 'Everybody' and could have been shot anywhere in the world, but everyone agreed it was best to get them out of the way now, so the boys could complete the new album and then concentrate on the master plan: to conquer America.

The Backstreet Boys had been lapping up success in far-off countries around the world for two years, but they were still unknown in their own back yard. Amazingly, they could come home from a sell-out tour of Germany, where their mere presence in a town would create mass hysteria, and walk around without prompting so much as a double-take from passers-by. It was hardly surprising; their début single 'We've Got It Goin' On' had sunk without a trace in the States and the boys had not bothered releasing a single since then. But a lot had changed in American music tastes in that time and the Spice Girls' success had proved that pop music was back in fashion.

While the boys were making their videos in LA, their record company Zomba began a strategy to break the boys in America by releasing 'Quit Playing Games (With My Heart)'. It was an inspired choice, because the melancholy love song that had been a global hit captured the imagination of the American market and its radio stations and became an instant sensation. It climbed to No.2 and became one of the most-played songs of the summer, giving the Backstreet Boys that much-needed breakthrough they had been longing for. The timing could not have been more perfect. As 'Quit Playing Games' rode high in the charts,

'Everybody' was released simultaneously around the world (except in America) and shot into the Top Ten in more than twenty countries, from the depths of South America, to Canada, Europe, Japan and East Asia. It sold 140,000 copies in its first week in Britain alone, taking it to No.3. The new single was a complete contrast to 'Quit Playing Games' and the other previously released ballads, and clearly demonstrated the depth of talent the Backstreet Boys had to offer. The pop world was blown away when they saw the stunning video. It was critically acclaimed and immediately caught the imagination of the fans, who made it easily the most requested video on MTV in Europe. For the Backstreet Boys, it was going to be a hot, hot summer.

Buoyed by the success of 'Everybody' and 'Quit Playing Games' in the States, the record company decided to give the Backstreet Boys' new album the biggest simultaneous international release in boy band history. There were actually two versions of *Backstreet's Back*. One was the international album, which was the group's second, and the other was a special compilation which counted as the American début album. The albums had more or less the same cover design, but featured slightly different tracks. The American edition had a 12-track 'super compilation' of the cream from both albums, to give the boys the strongest chance of success in the States. It

was a potent mix of early releases and the best of the new songs. The track list was: 'We've Got It Goin' On', 'Quit Playing Games', 'As Long As You Love Me', a specially extended version of 'Everybody', 'All I Have To Give', 'Anywhere For You', 'Hey, Mr DJ', 'I'll Never Break Your Heart, Darlin'', 'Get Down', 'Set Adrift On Memory Bliss' and 'If You Want It To Be Good'.

On Tuesday 12 August, more than 300 foreign and American music journalists, TV crews and record company people packed into the All Star Café in Manhattan, New York, for the press conference to announce the release of *Backstreet's Back*. Thanks to satellite technology, the events that day were not restricted just to those in the shadows of the skyscrapers, but were beamed live around the world. In London, the satellite link was set up in Football, Football, a new sports bar in the West End. Although there was no sporting

association with the day's events, the venue was perfect because it has a giant TV screen and countless monitors scattered around the restaurant. Executives from the UK branch of the record company, pop writers and a select group of the most loyal fans feasted on burgers and Mexican food as they prepared for the momentous launch. When the big screen finally crackled into life, a senior executive from Zomba started proceedings by announcing the Backstreet Boys' latest CD sales. He proudly told the audience that to date, the first album had sold seven million copies and the single 'Everybody' had already sold 1.2 million and had gone to No.1 in six countries. The demand for the second album had exceeded all expectations and more than five million copies had been distributed in advance orders alone. These figures already guaranteed the Backstreet Boys multi-platinum success without one day of promotional work. The sales figures and details of the album were interesting for everyone watching the press conference, but what they really wanted to see was the guys responsible for those mind-boggling statistics, not the men in suits. After that long corporate introduction, the charismatic Backstreet Boys finally took to the stage, looking cool in black jackets and brightly coloured shirts. And just in case anyone was unsure, they introduced themselves one by one.

Despite the expense and high-profile nature of the press conference, it did at times slip into farce, especially when some of the foreign journalists put inane questions to the boys or asked them to say 'Hi' to fans thousands of miles away. There were some embarrassing moments, but Brian broke the tension when he led a sweet *a cappella* snippet of 'Quit Playing Games'. By contrast, Kevin came out with a serious observation which clearly showed that the boys were far smarter than some might expect, especially given their sugar-coated images. During a reply to one question from the floor, Kevin said: 'We have learnt a lot about showbusiness. We know that there is the *show* and then there is the *business*.' These would prove to be deeply prophetic words.

Following the press conference, the boys dashed next door to the Virgin Megastore where they performed a short set, singing 'Everybody', 'Just To Be Close To You', 'As Long As You Love Me', and 'Quit Playing Games'. Unfortunately, it has to be said that this was not the best Backstreet Boys performance the world has ever seen. The group seemed hampered by the restricted space and struggled through their routines while singing to a backing tape. But, whatever mistakes the critical eye may have spotted, the press conference itself was considered a success, getting the album talked about and primed to sell many millions.

Straight after New York, the boys returned to Orlando, where life for them was set to change at an alarming rate. In previous months, they could easily have gone unnoticed locally – and just about anywhere else in America, for that matter. Occasionally, they were stopped by a rare American fan who had followed the group's success by buying imported CDs, and it was not uncommon for fans from abroad to track down the boys' homes while on holiday from Germany or Britain. However, thanks to the success of 'Quit Playing Games' and the hype surrounding the new album, things were already different and the group's popularity was snowballing by the day. The guys weren't exactly mobbed everywhere in the States as they were in Europe, but they were spotted more frequently and one of the first indications of change came with an impressive turnout for a signing session in one of Orlando's shopping malls. The Backstreet Boys were fast becoming stars in their hometown

and it was obvious that soon the privacy they had taken for granted there would be gone forever. It was a frightening prospect, but the boys had to accept that they were now on the way to becoming genuinely global celebrities.

Once back in Florida, the guys began working out in the gym and the dance studio, rehearsing flat out for a summer tour of open-air concerts in stadiums across Germany. It would be their biggest tour to date and it needed immaculate planning and tight choreography. Their dance coach Fatima, who has been with the group since the beginning, had several new routines worked out for them and she put them through their paces until everything was memorised and step perfect. The boys didn't even get the chance to rest during the breaks from dancing — instead, they had to team up with their backing musicians to get the set rehearsed. The workload during these days of preparation for the trip to Germany would prove to be typical of the punishing schedule that lay ahead for the Backstreet Boys during their world tour to promote the new album.

Once they were ready, the boys and their crew flew to Germany for three days of technical run-throughs to fine-tune the lighting and sound system before the final dress rehearsals. At the hotel, the guys were joined by the new support act for the tour – Nick's hyper-active younger brother, Aaron, who was beginning to make a name for himself as a rising young pop star. Aaron immediately made his presence felt, as Brian revealed: 'We knew Aaron was in town because we heard him screaming and running up and down the hotel hallway. Then he came round the corner screaming, "Nick, Nick, Nick".'

The opening night of the tour was in Hanover on 22 August – a double celebration, as it fell on Howie's twenty-fourth birthday.

Some might consider it tough having to work on your birthday, but when your job involves singing to 28,000 screaming fans, surely there can be fewer more exciting ways to toast another year. The night in Hanover was truly memorable, as the guys dazzled their fans with a series of costume changes and funky dance routines to a pulsating set of the best new and old Backstreet Boys songs. Brian impressed everyone when he played guitar for a solo spot, singing his moving self-penned love song, 'That's What She Said'. AJ unveiled his latest hair colour – bright yellow – and made the crowd laugh by whizzing across the stage on a motorised crimson armchair. And all the on-stage action was skilfully punctuated with a colourful fireworks show. Hanover was a triumphant night and it marked the beginning of a hugely successful thirteen-date tour, which saw the Backstreet Boys greeted by scenes of mania in every major city across Germany.

Away from the stage, however, not everything ran so smoothly. During one overnight stop, Brian had $150 in cash stolen from his hotel room. It turned out that a staff porter had sneaked into the room and taken the money, but luckily he had been spotted by one of the group's security men. The money was recovered and the porter was duly sacked. On another occasion, the boys had a fright when their small private jet had to make an emergency dive to escape a violent electrical storm. Neither of these minor mishaps detracted from the fun of the tour and, as it drew to a close, the guys relaxed with a charity basketball game in front of an 18,000 crowd. They played against their aspiring pop rivals N Synch, who were already gaining a

following in Germany. All the Backstreet Boys love basketball; they insist on taking a hoop with them wherever they are touring and can be seen fooling around with the ball backstage and on their rare days off. All that practice certainly paid dividends during the big game. Although N Synch are good friends and under the same Florida management team, it was a fiercely competitive match, but the Backstreet Boys made sure their superiority in the music world was reflected on the basketball court and chalked up a comfortable victory. With barely time to cool down after the game, the guys were on a flight to London for three days to promote the new single, 'As Long As You Love Me', with press interviews and key appearances on *Top of the Pops* and the *National Lottery*. They were delighted to see the single rise to No.3 in the charts and returned to

Orlando satisfied and ready for a well-earned five-day break.

O nce the boys had recovered from their jet lag and general exhaustion, it was time to hit the road again and begin their first serious tour of America. The Backstreet Boys had clocked up thousands of miles around the States in the years before they were famous, doing what is known in the music business as 'seeding' – that is, introducing themselves to new audiences and sowing the seeds of their music, even though they did not have a record in the shops back then. They had performed at schools and under-18 nightclubs with an aim to reap the rewards sometime in the future. Well, that time had come. The new album was

selling well and their second release in America – 'As Long As You Love Me' – had hit the No.4 spot in the Hot 100. With their fan base in the States growing at such a rapid rate it was clear the time was right for harvesting their rewards with some quality live shows.

The boys were not yet at the level to fill arenas, so they set off on a mini eight-date tour of modest-sized venues. Significantly, the first show was in Orlando, the home of the Backstreet Boys. It was here that they had taken their first tentative steps to fame four years earlier in Lou Pearlman's dream plan. It had been a long and tiring struggle with many disappointments along the way, but at last the boys were able to perform for their home crowd with a degree of Stateside success under their belts. A small local following had built up in Orlando over the years, thanks largely to the Internet and imported CDs. There had also been a lot of talk about the group, but most of it had been pretty dismissive. Because the Backstreet Boys' initial success had happened so far away, it seemed to many as if it didn't really count. Gold and platinum records across Europe, No.1 hits, sell-out tours, millions of fans – and they still heard, 'Hey, so what guys, you ain't nothin' in the States.' Well, thanks to their chart hits in the US, the Backstreet Boys did matter now and the Orlando concert was a chance for the boys to show the doubters they were a talented pop group who could cut it live. However, as AJ revealed, the group still felt some trepidation about the concert and the tour generally. 'You really don't know what to expect,' he admitted. 'Even though this is home for us, it's still a new territory and you don't know what the reaction will be.'

An extended entourage of the Backstreet Boys' relatives, close friends, behind-the-scenes helpmates from the earliest days, and the growing number of loyal local fans crammed into the Orlando venue to see the hot new boy band in action. And they weren't disappointed. AJ had nothing to fear: it was a night of triumph in Orlando and the guys were up and running across America. From there, they travelled north to Philadelphia and for two other dates along the east coast before heading to Chicago and Detroit. The guys only performed to crowds of 3,000 or so at each destination, but this represented the next level of 'seeding'. With each show the buzz about the Backstreet Boys grew louder and, by the time the curtain fell at Irving Plaza, in New York on 30 September, the boys knew the next tour would be bigger and better.

As the Backstreets unwound after the concerts, they reflected on their return to the States. Nick said: 'We always wanted to bring it back home – but we wanted to make sure we brought it back strong. We've done that. Now we're ready for everyone to come and mob us!' And Brian acknowledged the Spice Girls' part in helping the boys to crack America. He said: 'I think a lot of it has to do with the Spice Girls bringing pop back into the US. They started getting successful and everybody in America turned round and said, "OK, where are the great home-grown acts?" So we turned up and said, "Here we are. We've been here all along, you just never noticed us before." It's great to have the recognition at home. It took a long time, but finally our fellow Americans have cottoned onto us.'

AJ added: 'I'd say this is a big dream come true. We'd never really gotten the chance to be here for the last year and a half. Now we're finally bringing it home. We wanted to release the album a lot sooner, but it just took off in Europe and everywhere else, so we decided to go there first. I'm kind of glad that it happened the way it did, because we got the chance to hone our craft.'

Kevin was clearly still awestruck by the group's success: 'The whole thing is a dream,' he confessed. 'I'm just happy to have a job that I love to do . . . When I was little, I grew up dreaming about singing in front of thousands of people and I'm getting to do it. The fact that we're performing in the United States where all my friends and family can see what is really going on has got me very excited.'

Finally, Howie gave a mature outlook on what was happening to the boys in America.

He said: 'I think the market is more ready for a group like us now. When we released our first record, grunge and urban music were hot. Now we feel that pop music is coming back a little. We're being compared to New Kids and Spice Girls, which is a compliment. We used to come home and no one would recognise us, but now we get stopped the whole time. Somehow I don't think life will be the same any longer.'

How right he was, though his words would prove to be a mighty understatement. The Backstreet Boys were well and truly back!

the loneli

ness
of
stardom

Soon after the début US tour, the guys headed back to Europe where their popularity was bubbling up like crazy. The new album had been a sure-fire hit and 'Everybody' had been played so much on radio that it had won the group a whole new range of fans. An older generation was getting into the song, which in turn considerably boosted the boys' credibility within the music industry and made people start to take them more seriously. But, most importantly, the Backstreet Boys' teen fan base across Europe was soaring, thanks to the new album, which had gone platinum in a dozen countries. In Spain alone, *Backstreet's Back* went eight-times platinum with 800,000 copies sold and it sparked renewed interest in the first album, which by now had gone four-times platinum. This escalation in the Backstreet Boys' popularity was clearly evident when the boys flew to Madrid in early October for a free charity concert. The organisers chose an area in the old part of the city and felt confident that space for 2,000 fans would be sufficient. Five hours before the boys were due on stage, the area was already packed solid and thousands more fans were on their way. It was a disaster waiting to happen and before long the authorities had to admit they had grossly underestimated the attraction of the show and were forced to cancel it for fear of fans being crushed. For the Backstreet Boys to appear in Spain with their current popularity, it was probably best to allow room for at least 15,000 fans.

The Madrid situation was a clear indication of just how much the Backstreet Boys' fame had exploded in recent weeks. There were now even more girls waiting outside hotels wherever the guys stayed, which led to an increase in security problems. The boys' security team were now up against more fans trying to get near the boys and the increase in competition meant that the girls were having to be more imaginative. The hotel switchboards were carefully briefed not to put any calls through to Kevin or the other lads unless they were certain they were genuine. A hotel operator can literally take hundreds of calls from fans claiming to be distant relatives, girlfriends or sisters of the boys. Some are so convincing that they do get through to their idols and a girl posing as one of Howie's sisters did her research and American accent so well she was connected to his room. Howie was so impressed by her determination that he chatted happily with her for a while. Groups of girls frequently check into an expensive hotel and cram eight or more into a single room to share the costs. Once on the inside, they have free access to other floors and the internal phones, but that doesn't mean it is any easier to meet the boys. They normally stay on the executive floor of a hotel and their security make sure the lifts are watched carefully to stop any unwanted visitors. Even girls posing as staff need to be able to perform at drama school level to stand a chance of getting past the various checkpoints.

The downside to the added fame for the Backstreet Boys was the sudden attention of the paparazzi. A few months earlier the boys had been of little interest to the freelance photographers who prey on celebrities, but now there was good money to be made out of them. Whenever they ventured out of their hotels in Spain, Germany or Italy, the boys could be certain they were being secretly followed. It was harmless most of the time, but there was one incident when they were harassed by a photographer in a Spanish nightclub which proved particularly annoying. Kevin revealed: 'We work pretty hard these days, so we need to go out and party sometimes. When I choose to go out and have a good time, then I'll do it, as long as it's in a responsible way. The only thing we have to worry about are the paparazzi. It's like, me, AJ and Howie went to a club and these photographers kept hounding us, so our security said they could take a picture then leave. But they weren't happy with that, so they ended up printing a story in the paper the next day about AJ getting into a fight, which was completely fabricated. I guess people just love to gossip.'

This sort of problem was a minor inconvenience when you consider the exciting lives the Backstreet Boys were leading. Their time throughout the autumn months of 1997 was filled with jetting back and forth across the Atlantic for various promotional appearances and shows. They celebrated Hallowe'en in Chicago by teaming up with Hanson for a live radio broadcast, then flew back to Europe for the MTV Awards where they performed 'As Long As You Love Me' and made a slice of pop history when they became the first group to win the phone-in MTV Select Award for the second time. They beat firm favourites the Spice Girls that day and the turnaround in fortunes for the two groups was evident again at another awards bash in Spain soon after the MTV party. Here, the girls were booed by the audience of press and VIPs for refusing to perform until photographers were cleared from the auditorium. It was the beginning of a temporary backlash against the rise of Girl Power and it was rubbed in further when a short while after the girls left the stage somewhat bemused and embarrassed, the Backstreet Boys were greeted with cheers. It was a clear lesson in the fickleness of pop.

The awards, accolades and CD sales continued to pile up and while they were back in New York taking part in a Thanksgiving Day parade, the boys learnt that *Backstreet's Back* had already gone gold in the States and was on target to turn platinum with one million sales. A platinum disc in America had been their dream prize since the beginning of the group and it seemed that each new day brought the passing of a landmark that had once been some far-off fantasy. This was perfectly illustrated at the annual *Smash Hits*

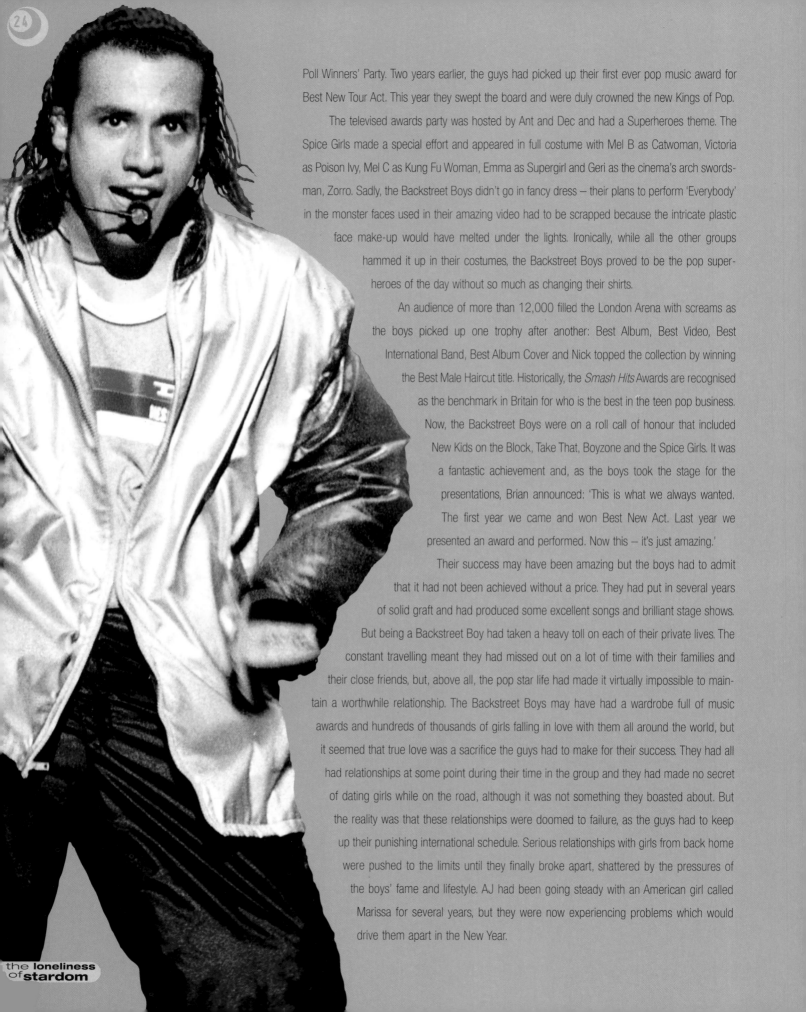

Poll Winners' Party. Two years earlier, the guys had picked up their first ever pop music award for Best New Tour Act. This year they swept the board and were duly crowned the new Kings of Pop.

The televised awards party was hosted by Ant and Dec and had a Superheroes theme. The Spice Girls made a special effort and appeared in full costume with Mel B as Catwoman, Victoria as Poison Ivy, Mel C as Kung Fu Woman, Emma as Supergirl and Geri as the cinema's arch swordsman, Zorro. Sadly, the Backstreet Boys didn't go in fancy dress – their plans to perform 'Everybody' in the monster faces used in their amazing video had to be scrapped because the intricate plastic face make-up would have melted under the lights. Ironically, while all the other groups hammed it up in their costumes, the Backstreet Boys proved to be the pop superheroes of the day without so much as changing their shirts.

An audience of more than 12,000 filled the London Arena with screams as the boys picked up one trophy after another: Best Album, Best Video, Best International Band, Best Album Cover and Nick topped the collection by winning the Best Male Haircut title. Historically, the *Smash Hits* Awards are recognised as the benchmark in Britain for who is the best in the teen pop business. Now, the Backstreet Boys were on a roll call of honour that included New Kids on the Block, Take That, Boyzone and the Spice Girls. It was a fantastic achievement and, as the boys took the stage for the presentations, Brian announced: 'This is what we always wanted. The first year we came and won Best New Act. Last year we presented an award and performed. Now this – it's just amazing.'

Their success may have been amazing but the boys had to admit that it had not been achieved without a price. They had put in several years of solid graft and had produced some excellent songs and brilliant stage shows. But being a Backstreet Boy had taken a heavy toll on each of their private lives. The constant travelling meant they had missed out on a lot of time with their families and their close friends, but, above all, the pop star life had made it virtually impossible to maintain a worthwhile relationship. The Backstreet Boys may have had a wardrobe full of music awards and hundreds of thousands of girls falling in love with them all around the world, but it seemed that true love was a sacrifice the guys had to make for their success. They had all had relationships at some point during their time in the group and they had made no secret of dating girls while on the road, although it was not something they boasted about. But the reality was that these relationships were doomed to failure, as the guys had to keep up their punishing international schedule. Serious relationships with girls from back home were pushed to the limits until they finally broke apart, shattered by the pressures of the boys' fame and lifestyle. AJ had been going steady with an American girl called Marissa for several years, but they were now experiencing problems which would drive them apart in the New Year.

It was a crazy contradiction that five of the most adored young men in the world often suffered from acute loneliness. Kevin, in particular, was seeking a meaningful relationship. As the eldest and generally the most serious of the group, Kevin yearned for the stability of a full-time girlfriend, not a fling on tour with a girl he would never meet again. Kevin comes from a family built on strong traditional values and deep down he was longing for the day he could marry and start a family. He had turned twenty-five on 3 October and was beginning to reflect on the conflict between his pop career and his desire to settle down and become a dad. He confessed: 'It's tough not being able to have relationships. When we're out on the road we have each other, but it can get lonely. Occasionally, we'll party and maybe meet someone and try to date them. We also try to date girls when we're back home. It's not easy, but that's just the way it is. The loneliest times are when you're lying in your hotel bed late at night and you wish you had someone there to cuddle and watch TV with you. I miss the everyday relationship-type things.

'I've been guilty of saying I'll phone a girl and then don't. I'll get home and mean to call, but our schedule is so hectic that I've just fallen asleep! Girls don't believe me, but it's the truth. I'm really looking for a serious relationship at the moment, so that someone is there for me. I want to have a family of my own and settle down one day. I come from a big family and I love kids. Every time I see a baby, I'm like, "Aaaaaah". When I was at the airport one day, a lady asked if I'd have my picture taken with her baby because I was playing with her so much. Yeah, I definitely want a family someday and it's just a matter of time before I get married and settle down.'

While the guys may have struggled to find the girl of their dreams, there was to stop them dreaming of the type of girl who could win their hearts. Not surprisingly, the Backstreets all have different tastes and expectations, but they all agree that they hope to find a girl who will love them for being themselves, not for being pop stars. 'My idea of the perfect girl is someone who likes to have fun and enjoy life,' Howie mused. 'I'm a very free and loving guy and I just try to have fun with life and not take it too seriously. I want someone who has a good head on her shoulders too – someone with her own career goals, who knows what she wants in life and is serious about getting it. She has to be a good communicator. For me, communication is a big thing in a relationship. You have to be able to talk. Without it there is no relationship.'

Brian, too, is looking for an independent girl. He revealed: 'I'd like someone intelligent who wants a career for herself and who is interested in achieving other goals in life. I'm looking for a very giving person, someone who's open and trustworthy and willing to have fun. She also has to be athletic, so we can go for a jog and lift weights together and have fun that way. For me, it's not about looks. I don't really have any specific physical likes – like redhead, blonde or brunette – but I do have to like a girl's eyes because they attract me. To me, eyes are very appealing.'

Beautiful eyes are important for Howie, too. 'I know most guys won't agree with me,' he said, 'but the first thing I look at in any woman is her eyes. When I look deeply into them, it's like "Wow!"

I also love a girl who has long fingernails because I like the way they feel on my skin. When a girl rubs the back of my neck with long nails – man, that's really nice! I'm not a picky kind of guy really, she just has to have a big heart and a sense of humour. I just want someone relaxed, someone I can be myself around, someone who doesn't make me feel I have to pretend to be someone I'm not.'

As for Nick, it was proving even more difficult for him to settle in a steady relationship. He joined the Backstreet Boys when he was twelve, so he had pretty much lived his entire adolescence in the group. When he was at school, he was mocked by lots of pretty girls because they thought his singing and dancing aspirations were uncool and they preferred to date the guys who were good at sport. Nick has never forgotten those days and is suspicious of glamorous girls who have thrown themselves at him since he has become famous. He tries to look beyond a pretty face these days, and has to be satisfied the girl is genuine before he is interested. 'She doesn't have to be someone who has everything you've ever dreamt of a girl having,' he revealed. 'But if she fits the characteristics that fit you and you like her a lot, well then, that's what I'm looking for. Just as long as she has a great personality and a good heart and she's really nice, I'll be satisfied.

'Occasionally it feels a bit weird that girls put me up on a pedestal and I can't figure out why they like me the way they do. I never really get time to talk to fans much these days as we're always being rushed off, so I probably spend more time with older girls, like other artists and people in the business. But I don't get time to date at the moment.

'It can get tough being on the road for so long, but we all look out for each other and the guys are always there to give me advice. They have already been through most of the things I'm going through, so they can help me like that. They're my brothers and they're always there to talk to.'

Whatever the pains of fame, the Backstreet Boys would be the last to complain about their lives, especially after the success they enjoyed in 1997. Soon after the night of celebration at the *Smash Hits* party they landed back in Florida for a rest and to spend Christmas with their families. The boys were already laden with the spoils of an amazing year, but they were delighted to be told by their record company that there was still one more prize to be collected before the year was over, and it was the biggest one to date: the platinum disc for *Backstreet's Back* in America. Four months after the release of what was their début album in America, the sales had easily soared past the million mark and were now heading for multi-platinum status. Many groups work for years and produce several albums without ever scoring platinum sales, so the Backstreet Boys' achievement cannot be overstated.

Four years earlier, Lou Pearlman, the Backstreet Boys' founder, had hired pop managers Johnny and Donna Wright to help steer the boys to the top. The husband and wife team had worked with the New Kids on the Block and knew what it took to turn a new boy band into a teen phenomenon. On the day the couple agreed to work with the Backstreet Boys, Johnny had handed Kevin and the other guys a framed platinum disc of the New Kids'

monster-selling album, *Hangin' Tough*, the record that had taken the New Kids to the heights of fame nine years earlier. Johnny told the boys to hang the record on a wall and look at it for inspiration whenever they doubted they would make it to the top. 'Don't take it down', Johnny said, 'until you can replace it with your own platinum disc.' There had been many times along the way when the Backstreet Boys felt they would never manage to emulate the boys from Boston. But now, as they prepared for the festive season, they could be forgiven for thinking that Christmas had come early for them. They already had the best presents of all, and at last they could take down the *Hangin' Tough* album. The New Kids were history; long live the Backstreet Boys!

new stars

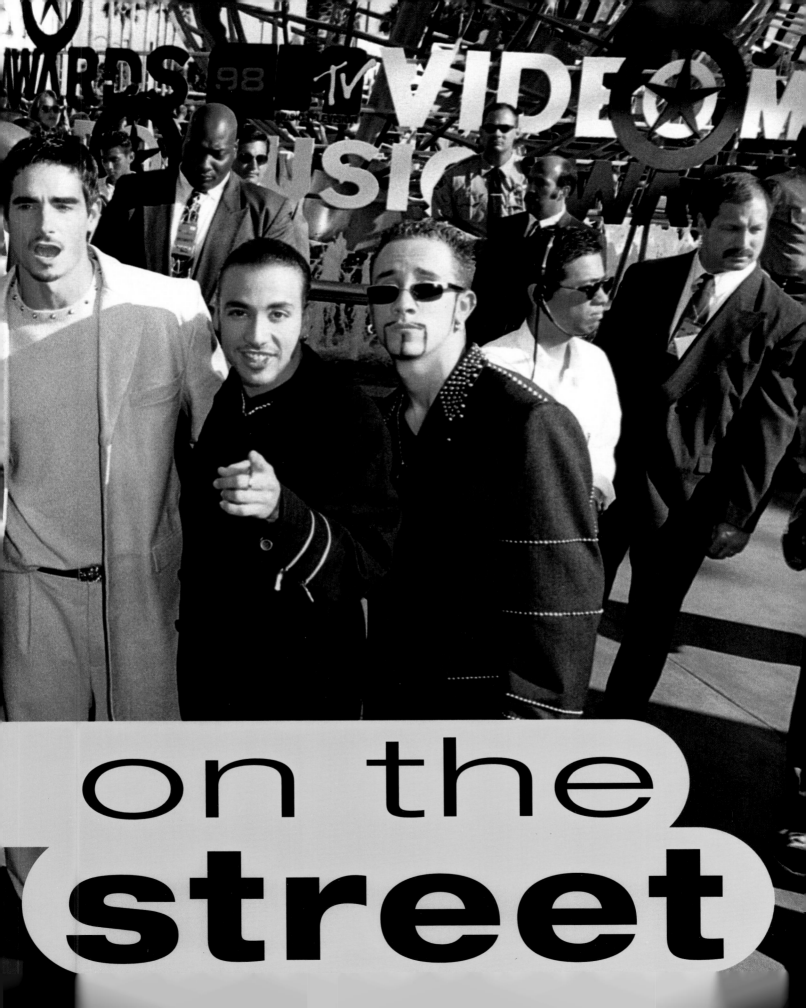

on the street

Soon after Christmas, the Backstreet Boys headed for one of the countries where they had first succeeded – Canada. From the earliest days of 'We've Got It Goin' On', the Canadian fans had been among the most enthusiastic in the world. An incredible 3,000 fans had turned up for the very first performance of that single in Montreal in 1995, and since then their fan base in Canada had mushroomed. The French province of Quebec proved to be the stronghold and, during a summer tour in 1996, the Backstreet Boys played to a staggering 65,000 at an outdoor festival in St Jean. Both of their albums had sold more than one million copies, which is a rare achievement in such a relatively small CD-selling territory, and even the compilation of the boys' videos had sold a million. This incredible swell of popularity had made the Backstreet Boys the No.1 act in Canada, eclipsing the country's own superstar, Celine Dion.

The main problem with travelling to Canada in winter was the bone-numbingly severe temperatures that engulf the country at that time of year. AJ, Howie and Nick are particularly sensitive to the cold having grown up in the Sunshine State of Florida, where having to wear a jumper in the middle of January is considered cause for complaint. Driving snow and freezing winds are not the boys' idea of fun, but at least they could be guaranteed a warm welcome from their fans wherever they appeared. Due to the time of year, the shows were confined to indoor arenas of 20,000-plus, which the Backstreet Boys could have filled many times over in every city. Tickets were so hard to get that it made them pretty much the hottest things in that part of the world!

The tour opened on 27 December in Halifax, Nova Scotia, on the far eastern coast and then moved to Ottawa, before arriving in Montreal for a big New Year's Day concert at the Molson Centre. Performing on such a day typifies life as a Backstreet Boy. While millions around the world are relaxing and trying to shake off the excesses from a night of celebrations, the five guys were sound-checking,

limbering up their shivering muscles and loosening their voices in preparation for a night's work. Working on birthdays and other annual celebrations has become a way of life for everyone in the group and their back-up team. The boys had not been home with their families for the traditional feast of turkey and pumpkin pie on Thanksgiving Day for three years – something they particularly missed. As for working on New Year's Day in Montreal, well, there were worst ways to start 1998 than being screamed at by 20,000 of your most loyal fans!

The Canadian tour continued from there to Toronto, then returned to Montreal for another show at the Molson Centre and a music awards ceremony, before closing in Quebec. It was a rousing end to a successful tour, and boosted the boys' confidence for the particularly gruelling tour of North America that awaited them. The immediate benefit was that the first leg began with five days in Los Angeles, which served as a recuperation and general thaw-out following the deep freeze of Canada. The guys were given two days off, which was something of a luxury, and they had a lighter schedule consisting of press and TV interviews and an appearance at the *Teen People* Party, the American equivalent of the *Smash Hits* Party.

Although the guys had made significant inroads into the American market with their chart hits, there was still a long way to go to reach the heights of popularity they enjoyed in Canada and Europe. The key to raising your profile in the States is television and getting invited on the big network talk shows. Although the boys were not able to fill a 20,000-seater

arena in the States just yet, the sales of the album and singles had drawn comparisons with the New Kids and the Spice Girls, which in turn assured them higher status for television promotion. While in LA, they did various inter- views for TV shows and newspapers, but the key promotion came on 9 January — AJ's twentieth birthday — when the guys were invited to sing 'All I Have To Give' on *The Jay Leno Show*, one of the hottest shows in the

States. It was a big break which introduced their sound and style to a nationwide audience of millions that would have been impossible to reach on the road.

Re-energised after their stay in LA, the Backstreet Boys headed east for Charlotte, in North Carolina, for the start of their whirlwind fifteen-date tour which would take them through thirteen states in nineteen exhausting days. A lot was riding on this tour: it was criti-

cal to maintain the momentum and capitalise on the group's success to date. It was also important to build on the foundations they had laid with that first tour a few months earlier. This time the boys were to perform in average- sized venues in big cities in the heartland of America, followed by high-profile concerts at prestigious theatres along the east coast and Florida. The tour was also significant to the boys on a personal level, because it would take

them all to places familiar from their roots and therefore serve as a kind of homecoming. The Backstreet Boys are known as a Florida band, which is why the Orlando gig had been so special, but Brian and Kevin are from Kentucky and they desperately wanted to take the Backstreet Boys back home. Howie, AJ and Nick also wanted to take the tour into their areas of Florida. All the guys had performed on home territory at some point before, but only in tiny venues, such as nightclubs or schools. This time, the boys would be performing a proper concert that would show their other relatives, and old friends they had lost touch with, what the group could really do. This personal desire to do well aroused a certain amount of anxiety in the boys. Brian revealed: 'We finally have an opportunity to focus on the US, which is very personal to us. We've worked very hard all over the world, so to come back here now makes me very nervous because you never know what the future holds.' Howie added: 'This is our home country and we've been waiting so long to come home. We took the backwards approach – going around the world, then coming back. But I think it was a good decision. We wouldn't change anything, because we got to see the world . . . We got a chance to go into these countries and actually see the culture and visit some of the really small cities. Now it's time to show America what the Backstreet Boys can do with a live concert.'

The next city after Charlotte was Atlanta, in Georgia, then Kevin and Brian got the chance to perform for their extended families and wide network of friends around Kentucky. The venue for the concert was at the Palace Theatre in Louisville, a sprawling city just a couple of hours' drive from Kevin's old hometown of Irvine and a similar distance from Lexington where Brian's family still lived. It may have been a short hop along the freeway for those friends to finally see for themselves what had become of the pop star cousins from Kentucky, but the boys' journey to that stage had been far longer. It felt like a lifetime ago that Kevin had sung his heart out on a tree-lined hillside in Irvine,

dreaming that he was entertaining an arena of fans. And it had been an age since the sweet sounds of Brian's voice had filled the Porter Memorial Church in Lexington, where he began his singing career as a choirboy. Whatever the emotional and geographical distance fame had driven between the two boys and their home state, it was still an amazing feeling for them both to finally bring a high-quality Backstreet Boys concert to their neck of the Kentucky woods.

From Kentucky, the group flew to the state of Michigan for a concert at the Fox Theatre in Detroit, then on to Columbus, Ohio, before it was Nick and Howie's turn to enjoy a homecoming concert in Tampa, Florida. The venue was not far from Nick's home in Ruskin on the banks of Tampa Bay, and it held a special significance for Howie because he had lived in the city while studying for an arts degree and simultaneously auditioning for acting and singing roles. He remembered all too well the rejections he suffered to get where he was. At one point he had even changed his name to Tony Donetti, in the vain belief that passing himself off as Italian might unlock an acting opportunity. Nick, too, had faced many struggles trying to break into showbusiness and he still remembered the tears he shed when school bullies and scornful girls derided his singing ambitions. Now Nick and Howie were back in Tampa, but this time as international pop stars with thousands of fans going crazy for them. It was a special feeling for both of them to be able to show their doubters that, against all the odds, they had made it.

After Tampa, AJ got his chance to show the begrudgers from yesteryear what he had

achieved, as the tour powered on to Florida's east coast for an appearance at the South Florida Fair in West Palm Beach. The group stayed in Boca Raton, the coastal town where AJ had spent the first twelve years of his life. It was in one of the town's shopping malls that the seven-year-old AJ took his first tentative steps to stardom, in a fashion show. His cheeky confidence won the audience over and his natural flair for performing was spotted by a local theatre director. She gave him his début stage role as Dopey in 'Snow White and the Seven Dwarfs' and it was from those humble beginnings that AJ entered a life of showbiz. Like Nick, he had been taunted by his sport-mad contemporaries because singing and dancing weren't cool, especially in a beach-oriented town such as Boca. The other kids had laughed when he didn't join in the baseball games because he was rehearsing for a new musical and they sniggered when he turned up at school carrying a briefcase and wearing glasses, even though he had perfect eyesight. Now, less than ten years on, that geeky oddball who had been such a figure of fun was striding back into town as a cool and self-assured pop star. The briefcase was long gone, but AJ still wore glasses and they were still only for show. These days, though, the glasses had become his pop star trademark and thousands of adoring fans screamed for him. Who was laughing now?

For all the Backstreet Boys, the first leg of this American tour was a personal journey that served as a statement to anyone who had written them off as hopeless dreamers over the years. It hadn't been enough to show people the CDs, or to talk about the success they

enjoyed thousands of miles away, or even about their rising record sales in the States. That all felt like fiction, or big talk, when it was relayed to people back in their home neighbourhoods. The Backstreets wanted those teachers who had shouted them down in class, the bullies who had laughed at them, and the pretty girls who had shunned them for the hunky quarter-back in the school football team, to see once and for all what they had achieved. It was indeed a sweet homecoming.

The few lucky fans who get to watch an adrenaline-fuelled concert see only a tiny polished segment of a Backstreet Boy's life. They see the lights and the costumes, and hear the screams and the music. But there is a much greyer, less interesting chunk to their lives that fills the long hours after the hysteria has faded. The shows are the fun and rewarding part of touring, but behind the glitz of a two-hour show, there lies twenty-two hours of draining pressures. There is the sheer exhaustion of constant travelling after no more than a few hours' snatched sleep; the mind-numbing boredom of waiting for planes, travelling by coach, and trying to be lively during monotonous press interviews in every city. And at the back of it all is the unsettling nature of living from day to day in hotels. Only after all the drudgery of getting from one country or city to the next are the two hours of fun possible.

Inevitably, it is the time between shows which produces the most tension. The Backstreet Boys are like brothers and they have lived and worked together almost continuously for five years, except for a few weeks' break once in a while. In those years, they have travelled hundreds of thousands of miles around the world and entertained an army of fans. Few brothers ever spend a fraction of that time together so, not surprisingly, the Backstreet Boys argue. When you consider that these five young men represent the golden tip of a multi-million pound industry, it is amazing that they have stayed together so long without any lasting fallouts, or personality clashes. As Lou Pearlman says: 'They hardly have any time apart, so it is remarkable just how well they all get along. They would have to be superhuman not to argue. They have more pressure than normal brothers, because they have to deal with fame and the music business generally. They cope really well and I am very proud of the way they have handled every new situation.'

AJ admits: 'We do fight and things happen between Nick and Kevin because there's such a big age gap. They have different views on things, but phew, it was worse when Nick was younger! There would be arguments about all sorts of things – what to wear, what music to play, what football team is the best – but it never came to blows, thank goodness. All we want is what's best for the group. We always try to talk things through and not let them fester.'

One of the reasons the Backstreet Boys work so well together is that although they have such different characters, they are cemented by a common bond – their love of music. Kevin is the mature, fatherly figure of the group; Howie is the calm peacemaker who sees every side of an argument; AJ – or Bone as the guys call him

– is the hyperactive showman who likes to party; Nick is the absent-minded boy who likes to mess around; Brian is a loveable joker but can also be very pensive and quiet. Nick and Brian – or B. Rok as he is nicknamed – are very close buddies and can often be found playing computer games or basketball together for hours on end when there's a chance. Howie calls them 'Flick 'n' Flack' because they are an inseparable double act.

Kevin is often mistaken for being miserable because he can be so serious, but he does have a lighter side. He says: 'I like to fool around like all the guys, but only when the time and place is right. I'm a perfectionist. I want things to be just right. We have rows sometimes because of that. Brian likes to play around, but he's got a serious side as well. Howie is very laid back and is probably the easiest going of the group. But we've all got a serious side, you gotta make time to be serious about what you're doing. AJ is very laid back as well, but talks a lot – especially with the women.

'Sometimes Nick's attention span is a little short, but I'm not sure if it is down to the age gap or just because of the kind of person he is. I like to work, get stuff done and *then* go and play, whereas Nick likes to work and play at the same time. We have very different personalities, but that doesn't cause massive problems or anything. Kevin Backstreet is very focused and hard working, but I like to goof off and play around when I'm not working. Sometimes I just need to hang out with my friends and get rowdy. When we're on the road, sometimes I hang out with the guys, sometimes I hang out with the band who are

all in their late twenties and thirties. They're all experienced musicians from all over America and they've got so many amazing stories to tell and a different type of conversation. I just love good company.

'There are times when I'm on the road and it gets frustrating. Sometimes I miss home, or I'll not be getting on with the other guys. It's not always easy and there have been times when I've thought, maybe this isn't for me, but the feeling fades and it all blows over. I think you need to go through times like that to appreciate what you've got.'

AJ chips in: 'Brian is the clown. Howie is a really sweet, suave character. Kevin is very professional and serious, yet with a very sensitive side. And me, I'm just crazy. We have less time off now so that puts us all under more strain, but it's been lots of fun and really worth it, even if it has taken a lot of dedication and patience.'

And Howie says: 'We all come from middle-class backgrounds and families of hard-working, wholesome people. We've all worked very hard to get where we are today and we appreciate very much what we have. We never take anything for granted. We know that we still have a lot of goals to reach. The lack of privacy can be tough, but it's not such a bad thing to have lots of screaming girls out there.'

Another mutual bond which has helped the Backstreet Boys stick together through the toughest times is their strong religious beliefs. They were all brought up to believe in God and an example of their faith can be witnessed backstage in the last private moments before a show. All the boys huddle in a tight group and hold hands with the key members of their entourage. Then someone is chosen at random to say a prayer out loud. It is not a rehearsed piece, but a spontaneous prayer to give thanks on behalf of everyone for all their blessings and continued good health. Anyone standing nearby remains silent and still until they hear 'Amen'. This pre-concert ritual has been followed before every Backstreet Boys show since their first gig on 8 May 1993 at Sea World in Orlando. It is a ritual that keeps them grateful and grounded and helps remind them of their history. When the prayer is over, the five boys have a final hug of solidarity to pump themselves up before following a body-guard with a torch light through the darkness to their opening positions on stage.

Following the Florida leg of their US tour, the boys moved up the coast for shows in Washington, then Providence, Rhode Island, and New Haven, Connecticut, before a mad twenty-four-hour dash to LA to present a trophy at the American Music Awards. After the ceremony they were straight back in the air, bound for New York. By this time, their national popularity had moved up a gear and the tour had gathered considerable momentum. Now a considerable wave of mania greeted the boys in every town. Kevin noticed that the reaction of the fans at the concerts was becoming more powerful with each venue. He said: 'At some of our shows, it seemed like we were in Germany. The crowds were going nuts. We were scared at times, because people were getting hurt and crushed up against the barricades. It gets kind of scary, but our security do a great job.'

Even Brian, a veteran of hundreds of performances, was overwhelmed by the feel-ing of playing in New York. The following morn-ing he said: 'Before the show, I was thinking I wasn't going to be nervous because we've done it fifty million times – I know it like the back of my hand. But right before the curtain dropped, I was thinking, "This is New York City!" And I mean, that's all you have to think about. Not only is this America, but this is New York City. I mean, how rough and tough can you get, or how American can you get? I clammed up for a second and then I heard the music and I calmed down and it turned out really well. We got a great response and I was really excited.'

The fans had even more to scream about at the second New York concert, because it fell on 28 January – Nick's eigh-teenth birthday. Nick, the one-time unpopular geek, smiled as thousands of girls sang Happy Birthday and yelled his name. He had another reason to look pleased with himself, because reaching such a teenage milestone meant he

no longer had to be chaperoned, or have a tutor on the road. It seems unbelievable, when you look at the life Nick had been living for so long and realise that only now was he being accepted as an adult.

Once the birthday celebrations were over, the boys got their heads down for two more stops before closing the tour at the Broncos' stadium in Dallas, Texas. As the lights went out on the last show, the boys looked back happily on a thrilling tour that had taken them to a new level in America. The meticu-lously planned itinerary had kept jet lag to a minimum, but it had been a mad nineteen days and they were looking forward to catch-ing up on some sleep in their own beds. Once back in Florida, however, they soon realised that their success in America was already proving a double-edged sword. Yes, they wanted the fame and the trappings it brought, otherwise they wouldn't have being working so hard in the States, but until then, their home country had been their last refuge of anonymity. Now they were well-known faces

to millions and among the new fans were some obsessive characters. Suddenly, the boys' families were targeted by fans and were dogged by phone calls from strangers at all hours of the night and even visits from girls who had driven hundreds of miles to find the places where the boys had grown up. Fans would frequently turn up at the Littrell or Richardson family homes in deepest Kentucky and Nick's parents were so plagued by visitors that they were forced to put up an iron fence around their house.

This new-found fame brought some unwanted worries. Kevin revealed: 'It was strange at first. Our popularity in Europe was so big and the number of fans was amazing. We would leave Europe and have a couple of hundred fans at the airport, then we would come home to the US and have no one know who we were. We used to fly home and be normal people, but now our music and popularity in the States is beginning to grow, so that gap is getting smaller and there are fewer places we can go and not be recognised. It's very exciting, but scary at the same time. My family have already been forced to change their telephone numbers and I'm worried my mom will have to move. The rest of my family think it's quite exciting and they're really cool about it, but I want my mom to keep her privacy. I just wanna make sure she's safe.'

As the Backstreet Boys learnt to cope with the difficulties of domestic stardom, there were still plenty of compensations, none more so than when the latest sales figures for *Backstreet's Back* came through. It had now gone double-platinum in America and was rising by the day.

chapter four

the trans

48° FESTIVAL DELL
DI SA
backstreet boys
BACKSTREET'S BACK
4 PLATINUM DISC

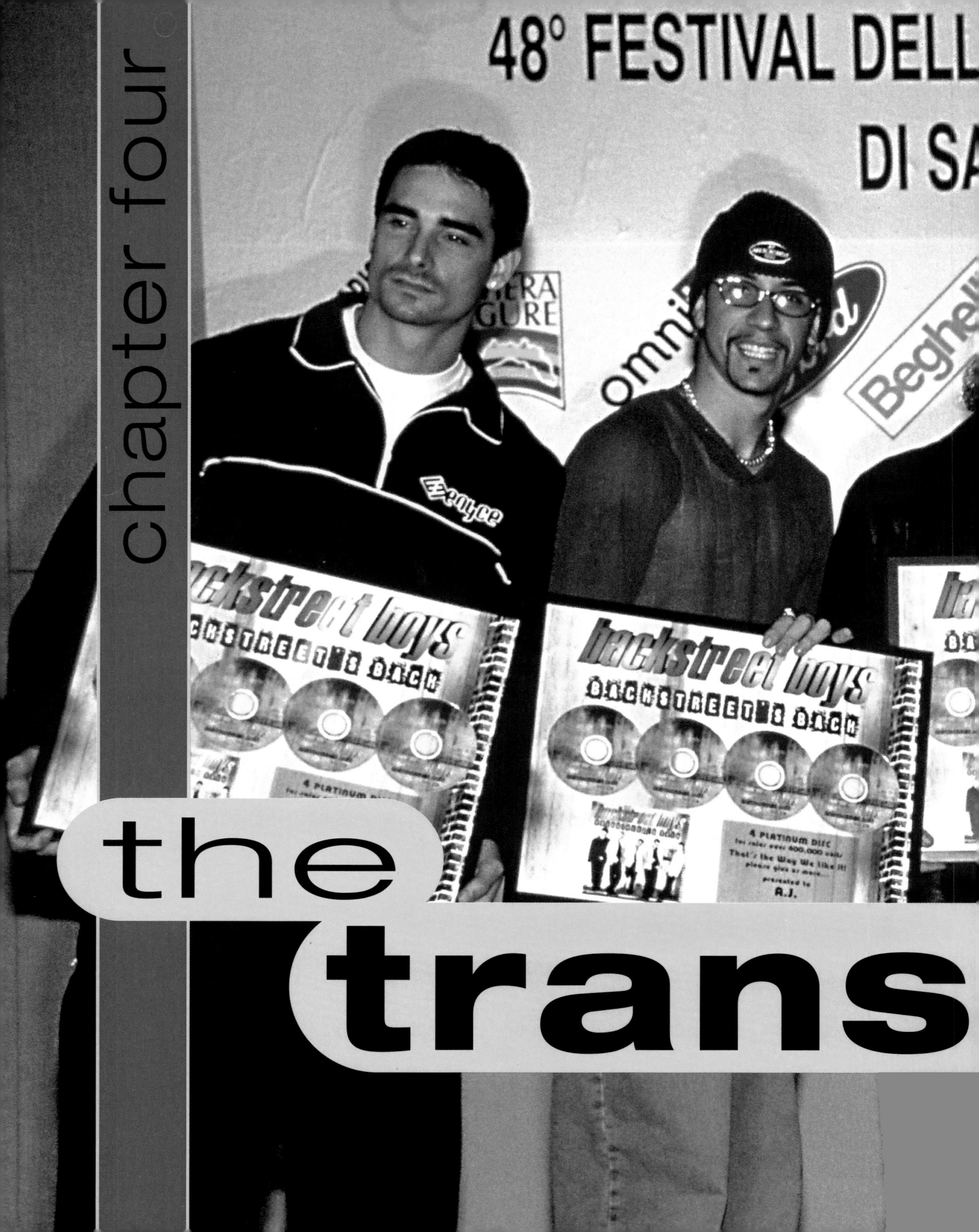

CANZONE ITALIANA

NREMO

atlantic
shuttle

Compared to the hectic schedule the boys had slogged through during the start of the year, the pace eased up slightly throughout February. There was still plenty of travelling to do, but the emphasis was on promotion, not full live concerts. So, after a short break in Orlando, the boys jetted to Germany for a three-day jaunt, principally to appear at the Bravo Super Show party where they performed five songs. This was followed by another break in Orlando before flying to South America for a show in Chile and TV appearances in Argentina, where the guys' popularity had just taken off. Howie came into his own in this region by speaking fluent Spanish throughout all the interviews, and it was clear that he could have a successful solo career in this part of the world some time in the future. The guys were so touched by the reception they received in South America that they started planning to release specially recorded Spanish versions of their songs, even though it meant everyone except Howie taking a mini-crash course in the language.

The next few weeks were filled with photo shoots for American teen magazines, TV promotion and general recuperation in Florida in the build-up to the next major European tour.

There was good news from England, where the new single 'All I Have To Give' rocketed to No.2, but this was easily eclipsed when their record company reported that the album had gone quadruple-platinum in America! When the boys flew to Italy in the closing days of February to perform at the San Remo music festival, they were each awarded a framed memento with four platinum CDs of *Backstreet's Back*. Now the boys were soaring way above landmarks set by the New Kids.

From Italy, the guys made a networked appearance on French TV in Paris before jetting back to Orlando. These short hops to Europe sound like fun, but the jet lag the boys

suffer is horrendous and they are constantly battling against disorientation caused by lack of sleep. They all take an array of different vitamin supplements to keep them healthy and AJ regularly resorts to sleeping pills to knock him out during long flights. As for Nick, he can sleep anywhere and has no problem crashing out wherever he can rest his head.

On returning from Paris, the group had seven straight days off which gave them plenty of time to get over the jet lag. But they had to make the most of the rest of their time off, because it would be their last decent break before the next marathon leg of their world tour began. For Brian, however, there were some

serious health matters to attend to before he could consider work again. Unknown to the fans who had enjoyed his recent stage performances, he was having worrying heart problems. Brian was born with a hole in the heart and over the years he always had regular check-ups to monitor its condition. During a recent consultation, his specialist was concerned that it had become fractionally larger, probably aggravated by Brian's hectic and energetic pop star lifestyle. The doctor insisted an operation was necessary and that Brian would have to be extra careful about his health in the immediate future. The operation was relatively simple by today's standards and would be performed by a top specialist, but the news was a major blow for everyone. It came just as the Backstreet Boys had caught the tip of a tidal wave of success, but everyone was in no doubt that CD sales and concerts were of no significance compared to someone's health. At least the doctors said that nothing had to be changed on the schedule for now and that he could go ahead with the European tour. But it was agreed to clear the workload once those dates were completed, so he could have the operation and a full month to recover afterwards.

With the prospect of the operation hanging over him, Brian eased himself back into work on 8 March. He joined the other guys for a few days' rehearsals in Orlando for the songs they were to perform for a televised unplugged concert to be screened in Germany later that month. Once they had worked through that set, they were off to the Caribbean for a sun-soaked, beach-side performance for MTV's special Spring Break show in Jamaica. The guys donned cool combat trousers and sun hats as they gave the reggae-loving local Rastas a taste of pop music Backstreet-style. After the show, the guys flew to New York to sing on *Saturday Night Live*, another top-rated show in America, and the following morning they were straight back to Orlando for a press conference before an evening flight to Ireland, where the European tour would start. As they jetted off, AJ left with a heavy heart after a tearful break-up with Marissa. In the face of another tour, it was obvious that his life as a pop star was too crowded to accommodate a serious relationship. AJ said simply: 'It just didn't work out, but I'm trying to look forward and get on with things.'

The Backstreet Boys stayed in Dublin for three days to perform two road shows, the biggest being on 17 March for the St Patrick's Day celebrations. Fatima Robinson flew out to fine-tune some of the dance routines for the tour. Despite the jet lag and tight schedule, AJ, Howie and Kevin got the chance to taste the crazy nightlife of the Irish capital. They headed for the town's trendiest nightclub, The POD, a frequent hang-out for local stars like Boyzone, and surprised a few people who had heard about the group's clean-cut image by partying well into the small hours. Kevin told one onlooker: 'We're letting off a bit of steam. We've been working really hard getting the show right and we thought we'd party tonight.'

At least the guys had a day off to rest any Guinness-induced hangovers before the short flight to Birmingham for the beginning of the UK tour on 20 March. This was the group's first appearance in Britain since their clean sweep at the *Smash Hits* Awards three months earlier and, much to the disappointment of the fans, it was not to be a long stay. The boys were only due to play three dates and tickets had sold out within hours some months before. Demand had been so high that an extra matinee concert was laid on at Wembley Arena to make sure not too many fans were let down. The tour opened at the NEC on the outskirts of Birmingham where more than 15,000 fans filled the air with enough screams to prove that the UK boasted some of the most loyal Backstreet Boys fans. And those screams didn't go unrewarded. The show opened with a blast of fireworks and from there the boys

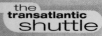

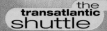

blitzed the audience with a stunning musical and dance display that matched the colour and excitement of any bonfire night celebrations. The fans were left spellbound by storming versions of the group's greatest hits from the early days with 'We've Got It Goin' On' right through to 'Everybody' and balanced the up-tempo songs with soulful ballads including 'Quit Playing Games', 'As Long As You Love

Me' and 'I'll Never Break Your Heart'. The guys also surprised the fans with some new songs and by taking it in turns to perform solo spots. The whole show was a sophisticated mix of skilled choreography and great pop music which left even the music press praising the Backstreet Boys. By the time they had completed the double-header of two shows in one day at Wembley, the guys had gained a new level of respect for their stage shows in the UK. While staying in London, hundreds of girls besieged their hotel and the group's security had to secretly arrange decoy cars to avoid a crush when the guys went shopping.

There was just one day off to pause for breath after Wembley before the gruelling section of the central European tour kicked off in the Danish capital, Copenhagen. During the next four weeks the Backstreet Boys needed their passports on an almost daily basis, as they weaved their way through nine countries. Many of the journeys on this leg were made by road in a specially converted coach with sleeping compartments for the boys and a lounge area with a television and small kitchen. For the longer distances, the boys would fly ahead to get a decent rest in a hotel while the coach and the road crew caught up. Nick hates flying so much that sometimes he would stay with the roadies on the buses and catch up with the other guys later.

After the Copenhagen show, the boys played one night in Gothenburg, Sweden, and then travelled to Germany for the broadcast of their unplugged special in Cologne, which gave them the chance to show off their *a cappella*

skills to the maximum. From there, they performed for just one night in Oslo, Norway, before it was back to Sweden for two big concerts in the capital, Stockholm. The guys had a day off following those shows, but then they moved on to Holland for two shows in Arnhem, followed by two in Gent, Belgium. It was a ridiculously tight schedule and, as the air miles piled up, the boys' patience began to crack. Kevin complained of a strained voice and showed signs of a throat infection, a common ailment among tired singers. Brian was also feeling the strain, but more from anxiety about the operation awaiting him back in America than his actual physical condition. This was understandable, as hospitals held bad memories for him. When Brian was five, a minor cycling accident led to a severe blood infection which took him to the brink of death. He was in hospital for two months as doctors battled to save him. Brian's mum, Jackie, a devout Baptist, stayed by his bed constantly and prayed for his recovery. But Brian's condition deteriorated and when she saw the pain her son was enduring, she accepted he was going to die and prayed that God should take him without any more suffering. Amazingly, from that moment Brian began to get well, and the turn-around in his health has always been acknowledged by the Littrell family as a miracle. The traumatic experience stayed in Brian's memory and has deeply affected his outlook on life over the years.

He recalls: 'Everyone thought I was going to die, but it all changed after my mom started praying differently. I honestly believe it was a miracle that I survived. The whole experience affected me dramatically as I got older. I was

really close to dying, so I appreciated everything that bit more. I feel blessed to have had such a wonderful life since then.' Memories of those awful months in hospital eighteen years earlier haunted Brian, but he still managed to face his new medical ordeal with maturity, matched by an unbreakable faith in God.

On a more trivial note, as Kevin and Brian dealt with health problems, Nick was living up to his reputation as the untidiest guy in the group. One of his nicknames is Chaos because he always leaves the most mess on the tour coach, and no matter how short his stay you can guarantee that Nick's hotel room will look like a disaster zone. As AJ says: 'Nick's room can look like it has been hit by a tornado. Clothes everywhere, video games, food, candy bars, everything. It could be called the comfort-able lived-in look – but only if you could actually find the bed!'

Typically, AJ loves driving people crazy with his energy and constant chatter, but his wacky humour often takes the edge off a situation and his passion for partying keeps everyone amused. He gives a wry smile when he reveals: 'We all have our share of a reputation with the ladies, ooh yeah. I'm the one who

persuades everyone else to party, then every-one tries to talk me out of things in clubs. Do they manage? Ha! No, I do what I like. I'm out of control. I think people would be really shocked to know what we're like. I don't think it would make our fans like us any less – I just think they'd sit back and have a laugh. We're five guys – five *single* guys – and we get a little crazy sometimes. We party our little butts off!'

AJ's mum, Denise, is the Backstreet Boys' personal assistant and is on hand to make sure everything runs smoothly for them on tour. She is also constantly around to keep an eye on her son, but AJ says he doesn't mind, because she is more like a sister to him

and lets him run free. As well as Denise, Howie is on hand to act as peacemaker during any tense moments and is always available to be a wise listener when one of his buddies is going through a rough spell.

When you look at the schedule of the European tour it is easy to understand why the Backstreet Boys were beginning to feel drained. Their emotions were constantly being pulled to the extremes, from the physical exertion and adrenalin of performing, to the mind-numbing boredom of travelling; all against a background of sleepless nights. As 1998 wore on, the guys became increasingly weary and they began to look more closely at the long-term strategy of their careers. They had learnt a lot over the previous years about the music business and they could see alarming signs that they were probably being driven to the limits of their energy out of a panic to cash in. Traditionally, teen bands have a peak period of around three years, and the guys could sense some people behind the scenes weren't expecting them to last much longer. The Backstreet Boys saw the future differently and were convinced they had the talent to succeed beyond that predictable cycle. So, as this world tour continued, they realised that the time was fast approaching when they would have to take more control of their lives, or face the inevitable burn-out and a sad ending on the pop star scrap heap.

As AJ put it: 'Things have got to the point where I might as well not even have an apart-ment back home. I'm paying out of the butt in rent, but I'm never there. When we're on tour, we want to go home, but when we're home for, say more than three or four days, we start climbing the walls and want to get back on the

  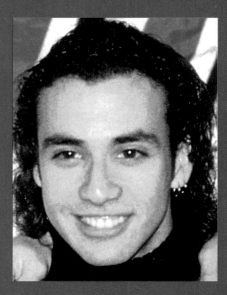

road. Sometimes it's like people don't realise we need time to eat and sleep.' Brian added: 'The schedule gets so monotonous. I kinda close up and don't say a lot. I think, "Hey, you gotta give us more time off. We've been working too damn hard – we're all gonna go nuts."

'I get frustrated so easily. It's not like I don't know how to chill out, but I have a really short fuse. I would really like my fuse to be a little longer. I've grown up a lot and I've developed a really business-oriented attitude. I was talking to my mom the other night and she was saying, "I'm very proud of the man you have become." I found that weird, because I don't think of myself as a man. I still feel like a kid.'

Whether there was a deliberate attempt to push the boys to their limits in order to cash in quickly is not known, but it was clear from the scenes that greeted the Backstreet Boys in every country that they were far from on a downward slide. They were gaining in popularity by the day and had reached such an altitude that it would take a long time for them to crash to the bottom. The same mad scenes of mass adulation followed the boys in every city across Europe. Devoted fans tracked down their

hotels and waited for hours just for a glimpse of the guys arriving and leaving. Some girls in cars even followed the tour bus for hundreds of miles as it sped along the various motorways to a new city. All the time, the bodyguards were kept busy trying to outwit the fans, but even the simplest everyday things became a hassle. If ever AJ fancies his favourite food, McDonald's, he always has to take a minder with him or risk being cornered by fans. The guys actually want to spend more time chatting to their fans, but they are constantly moved on by their security personnel for fear a crush will start and people will get hurt.

After Belgium, the Backstreet Boys juggernaut hit the road to Metz in France and then moved on to Paris for one night before heading south to Spain, which was firmly in the grip of Backstreet Boys fever. Scenes of mania on a par with Germany and the UK greeted the boys in Barcelona, Zaragoza, Valencia and Madrid. The final date of the tour was in Lisbon, Portugal, on 15 April, which was followed by a big celebration. As usual, AJ was the principal party animal after the curtain had come down. He said: 'We stayed out all night,

going from club to club, then having a party back at the hotel until ten the next morning. You have to force yourself to stay awake, but it's worth it. I passed out on the plane, though.' No need for sleeping pills this time!

Back in Orlando, the boys had an easy couple of weeks with six days off, followed by some teen magazine photo shoots and a big press conference at the Mariott Hotel on International Drive for the South East Asia media. After that, they flew to LA for two days to shoot a video and then returned to Orlando to record an Italian version of 'Quit Playing Games'. As soon as their finest Italian was in the can, it was time to speak French as the guys jetted out to the playboys' paradise, Monte Carlo, for a round of lavish parties and to sing 'All I Have To Give' at the World Music Awards ceremony. To be asked to perform at such a prestigious event was another indication of the respect the Backstreet Boys had earnt.

While the boys had been away on tour in Europe, the excitement about them had moved up another gear in America. The single 'Everybody' had finally been released there and had gone to No.4 in the charts. The video had

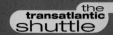

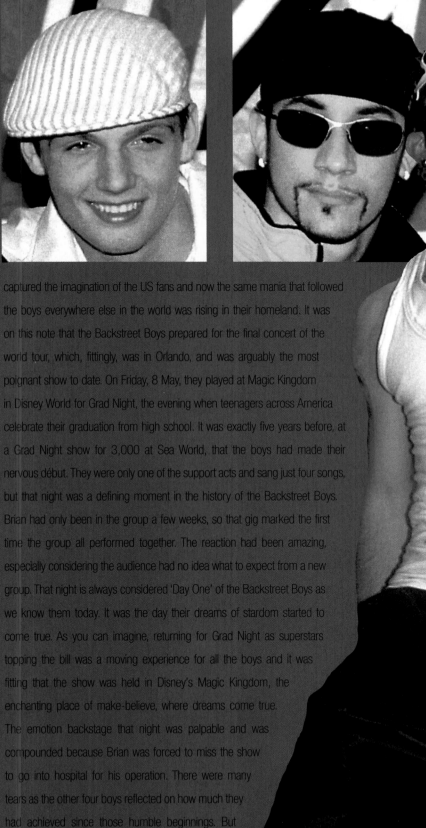

captured the imagination of the US fans and now the same mania that followed the boys everywhere else in the world was rising in their homeland. It was on this note that the Backstreet Boys prepared for the final concert of the world tour, which, fittingly, was in Orlando, and was arguably the most poignant show to date. On Friday, 8 May, they played at Magic Kingdom in Disney World for Grad Night, the evening when teenagers across America celebrate their graduation from high school. It was exactly five years before, at a Grad Night show for 3,000 at Sea World, that the boys had made their nervous début. They were only one of the support acts and sang just four songs, but that night was a defining moment in the history of the Backstreet Boys. Brian had only been in the group a few weeks, so that gig marked the first time the group all performed together. The reaction had been amazing, especially considering the audience had no idea what to expect from a new group. That night is always considered 'Day One' of the Backstreet Boys as we know them today. It was the day their dreams of stardom started to come true. As you can imagine, returning for Grad Night as superstars topping the bill was a moving experience for all the boys and it was fitting that the show was held in Disney's Magic Kingdom, the enchanting place of make-believe, where dreams come true. The emotion backstage that night was palpable and was compounded because Brian was forced to miss the show to go into hospital for his operation. There were many tears as the other four boys reflected on how much they had achieved since those humble beginnings. But there were also tears of sadness as their thoughts and prayers went out to Brian.

chapter five

the
show

and the
business

The Grad Night show brought a magical curtain down on the Backstreet Boys' world tour, but the happiest news came a day or so later when they heard that Brian's operation had been a complete success, with no complications. Hundreds of get well cards from fans poured in and the other boys went to see him when he was well enough to have visitors. Brian now had to take things slowly for many weeks and make sure he was strong again before he could consider getting back to his pop star life. He showed that none of his humour had been lost with the trauma of such an operation when he said, 'After resting I will join the band to finish recording our new album. Then it'll be Backstreet's Back!'

As for Kevin, Howie, AJ and Nick, it was time to take a proper step back from life on the road. The next two months of their schedule had been cleared for Brian's recovery and it allowed them some space to write songs individually for the next album and generally have a break from the confines of the group. They were able to slow down the pace and get some degree of normality back into their lives. They had a chance to spend some quality time with their families and open their minds up to fresh musical ideas. As much as they love their backlist of songs, singing them time and again gets tiresome. Nick admitted: '"Quit Playing Games" is about the only song I'm not sick of singing.' New material was long overdue, so throughout May and June the Backstreets linked up with various songwriters and musicians and laid down some ideas in the studio.

The boys found it was best to work separately at this stage because it gave them a chance to develop their own thoughts and avoid what would essentially be writing songs by committee if the whole group was involved. It was better to have a track ready and take it to the rest of the group later, for them to build on it with their input and harmonies.

As the guys worked on new songs, a whole team of people behind the scenes were planning a forthcoming tour of America. Incredibly, schedules were also being filled for up to a year's time to take in the release of the Backstreet Boys' new album and the next world tour. The guys were always looking to push the boundaries with each new tour, so things had to be planned way ahead. There were ideas to create a stage spectacular based on a medieval theme for the new tour, but a lot was to happen during those summer months which would throw all those plans into turmoil.

Taking a break from touring gave all the Backstreet Boys a chance to catch their breath and look at the wider picture of what they had achieved. While on the road, they lived a somewhat blinkered existence and kept their heads down to get on with the shows and be at their best as performers. But, as Kevin had said at the album launch almost a year earlier, they were fully aware that there was the 'show' and there was the 'business'. Now the shows were over for the time being, they were able to turn their full attention to the business side of the Backstreet Boys – and they didn't like what they saw.

The CD sales figures for the Backstreet Boys up until May 1998 revealed just how staggering their international success had been. Each release had reached gold or platinum status in every country you could imagine. The first album had gone gold in seven countries and platinum, or multi-platinum in twenty-three others. In just ten months, *Backstreet's Back* had gone gold in six countries and platinum or multi-platinum in thirty more, taking the total album sales past the twenty million mark. The group had also sold many millions of singles, but they account for a fraction of the profits in comparison and are mainly marketed by the record companies to drive sales of the albums. The figures spoke

for themselves and now the Backstreet Boys were eagerly awaiting the big pay day that would surely make them multi-millionaires. Unbelievably, this did not happen. And that's when the lawsuits started flying.

Some people might say it was inevitable that legal action would at some point blemish the sparkling success story of the Backstreet Boys. After all, that is the way things have turned out for so many big time music acts over the decades. Why should the Backstreet Boys be any different? But the benefit of pop music precedents certainly did nothing to

lessen the shock when the boys saw the net rewards for their superstar status. There was a long list of deductions: studio costs, songwriting royalties, marketing expenses, trade discounts, record company cuts, payments to their managers. The list went on and the cheque to the Backstreet Boys got smaller and smaller. The boys were not happy. Sure, they had become dollar millionaires, but they had made two blockbuster albums, filled hundreds of arenas and slogged their way around the world for five years, so they felt a million dollars or so each was not enough, especially when

you consider there was also tax to be paid. There were many tense meetings between the boys, their managers and the record company representatives, but, for whatever reason, a satisfactory settlement could not be reached. Finally, the boys decided to seek legal action. It was a sad day for everyone when the lawyers moved in and began what would prove to be a protracted and complex dispute that would embroil the boys for many months. It was a regrettable situation, especially considering everything the boys had achieved against the odds. Kevin was right when he observed drily: 'I think nowadays you've got to be business-men as well as musicians.'

While the legal bills escalated, the boys kept writing music and preparing for what they knew deep down was a bright future, no matter what the current problems. They did the occasional press interview and promotional appearance to keep the Backstreet Boys' profile high in America, but these were restricted to the bare minimum and did not involve the boys together. Howie completed a considerable amount of promo work on his own across the States, while Kevin, AJ and Nick pitched in with a few radio interviews and a charity basketball game in Arizona. Towards the end of June, Kevin had a break from song-writing to taste a slice of solo fame away from pop music – as a model. He flew to Milan, Italy, for a high profile fashion show and walked the catwalk for one of the top designers. Howie joined him on the trip to lend some support, but Kevin didn't need it. His natural stage confi-dence, complemented by his tall dark looks, sculpted torso and angular features, helped him make the transition from music to model-ling with comparative ease. The appearance of a teen pop star in Milan brought back memo-ries of Marky Mark's successful Calvin Klein underwear campaigns. Kevin's catwalk début was a success and it was clear there would be future opportunities for him in that line of work, should he want them. Whatever options lay ahead of him, Kevin gave a clear clue after the show that his ultimate ambitions lay in acting. 'In the entertainment business, everyone is so critical of what you look like,' he explained. 'I don't know if I'm entirely comfortable with my stage persona yet. I've got a sneaking suspi-cion that I'll come into my own playing an Italian gangster on the big screen.'

But life on the silver screen was some way off and for the immediate future, Kevin had to get back to his day job. As soon as he arrived back in the States with Howie on 1 July, they teamed up with the other guys for intensive rehearsals with choreographer Fatima Robinson for their first big all-arena tour of the States. Waiting to join them in the studio was Brian, full of life and raring to go. For someone who loves being active, he'd had enough rest to last him a lifetime and now he wanted to get back to singing and dancing. The guys had just six days to prepare for their first coast-to-coast tour, which would include thirty dates in twenty-four states. Everyone was a little rusty after such a long lay-off and they were eager to get back to full fitness. The days were split between working with Fatima on new choreo-graphy and with the band on the songs. The boys always aim to make their big shows a theatrical, as well as a musical spectacular, though this involves twice the amount of work. They don't just stand on stage and sing fifteen songs, but instead they create an extravaganza of complicated dance routines and costume changes, all smoothly blended with the music and special effects. To bring all that together in six days was a tough task and it involved twelve-hour days split between the dance moves and the music. If they were dancing until late at night, then the following morning they worked on the music, and vice versa. After six days, the guys had shed the few extra pounds they had gained during their time off and they were sharp again and ready for another gruelling tour.

As before, the tour began in Charlotte, North Carolina, but this time the show was in a 10,000-seater venue. Tickets for all the shows sold out within hours of going on sale and, if the boys needed any further proof that their popularity in the States had reached European proportions, they got it on this opening night and at every venue on the tour. The response from the fans was amazing and Backstreet-mania greeted the boys in every city. The boys unveiled a scintillating new show, but they also showed off some minor personal changes which illustrated their new feeling of maturity and desire for independence. Nick did away with his cute trademark centre parting which had won him the *Smash Hits* Best Haircut award and opted for a suave, greased-back look, while Brian grew some sideburns to give his baby face a more manly look. Not surpris-ingly, the most dramatic changes came from AJ who revealed some wild tattoos on his arms, much to the anger of the management.

AJ revealed: 'I was told off by the manager because he feared it would affect the image. But we're not about an image, we're about good music, so what I do with my body is what I do with my body. I just thought, "So what" – and I'm going to get another one!' However minor this rebellion may appear, it was a symptom of the control the Backstreet Boys wanted and felt they deserved.

From Charlotte, the boys and their crew headed to Florida for shows in Jacksonville and Miami before moving on to Atlanta, Washington and New York. Once they had taken a chunk out of the Big Apple, they made for the big cities in the central states, including Louisville, Detroit and Indianapolis, and in every city they were the sensation everyone was talking about. Everywhere the Backstreet Boys played, they were welcomed as heroes. The only slip-up on the way was when AJ twisted his ankle and had to miss a couple of shows before he was fully fit again.

It was clear from the success of the tour that the Backstreet Boys had scaled new highs and further proof of this came in the millions of dollars the fans were spending on T-shirts and other Backstreet memorabilia. The turnover of merchandise was on a scale not seen in American teen pop music since the New Kids on the Block. The coaches thundered on from one city to the next, and all the time the tills kept ringing and the boys kept singing. Dallas, Kansas City, Chicago, Milwaukee, Denver, Salt Lake City, they all seemed to merge into one until the boys finally arrived in Los Angeles. The final three dates in North America were San Francisco, Portland and Seattle, but, unbelievably, there was not even a day off before the

boys flew to Vancouver on 15 August to begin a coast-to-coast tour of Canada. They performed seven shows over the next ten days at traditional Backstreet Boys' strongholds, before conveniently ending up in Halifax, Nova Scotia, which led them seamlessly into more dates in New York and other cities on the east coast and finally back to North Carolina, where they had started nine weeks earlier.

The Backstreet Boys had been used to some hard tours before, but this one was up there with the toughest and it gave them first-hand experience of the vastness of their homeland. The only respite in the day-to-day grind came when they broke to fly to LA for rehearsals with Fatima, who had prepared a special new routine for them to perform at the MTV Video Awards. It was a glittering star-studded night and one to remember as the boys picked up the Best Group Video Award.

This award was one of the most coveted the boys had won, but the joy of victory was knocked into perspective a few days later by a terrible tragedy: Howie's sister Caroline died. Caroline was only thirty-seven years old, but she had been suffering from the skin disease lupus for some time. Her death devastated Howie and the entire Dorough family. He flew straight back to Florida to be with his parents, his remaining two sisters and brother Johnny. The Backstreet Boys still had three more shows left in the tour, but they postponed the next concert as a mark of respect for Caroline and the family. Flowers and sympathy cards flooded in from fans – indeed, such was the response that Howie set up a memorial fund at the Florida hospital where Caroline had been treated.

The Backstreet Boys' American tour finally came to a close on 15 September in York, Pennsylvania. After that show, the boys had some time off and were then honoured when the mayor of Orlando, Glenda Hood, announced she was granting Lou and all the boys the keys to the city as a reward for their incredible achievements. The mayor also declared that 8 October would be 'Backstreet Boys Day'. Anyone looking on at the pomp of the ceremony in Orlando could have been forgiven for thinking that everything was going brilliantly for the Backstreet Boys. That's how it might have appeared on the surface, but it was a different story behind the scenes. The legal wrangling between the boys, their record company and their managers was still rumbling on and there seemed to be no solution in sight.

The boys were soon due to begin recording their new album and a fourteen-date tour had already been booked in Germany from 1 December. But faced with the prospect of more work without a reasonable settlement, the Backstreet Boys decided to take drastic action. As much as they hated letting their fans down, they saw no alternative but to postpone the tour. The problems boiled over during the first few weeks of October and resulted in the boys sacking their managers, Johnny and Donna Wright. It was a hammer blow to the husband and wife team who had helped guide the boys to the top, but the working relationship had become intolerable. The dramatic sackings echoed the actions the Spice Girls had taken a year earlier when they fired the guru responsible for much of their success. The boys had seen the girls continue successfully without the aid of a manager and without having to hand

over 20 percent of their earnings. The Backstreet Boys had not been happy with the financial arrangements with Johnny and Donna, but they also wanted greater control over their working schedule and not to be driven to exhaustion. A pay-off to the couple was eventually negotiated, but from now on the boys would manage the group themselves, with Lou Pearlman continuing as their business manager.

The only remaining obstacle was the problem with the record company and the guys soon found the answer to that – they went on strike! The boys loathed resorting to such measures, but they were faced with few alternatives. How on earth could they record a third album while they were still unsatisfied with their wages for the previous two? Why should they continue blindly working themselves into the ground as world-famous pop stars unless they were going to be paid a top rate? As much as they loved their fans and the buzz of performing, who wants to work around the clock and soak up all the stress that goes with the job, unless you know it is going to pay dividends? It was a classic case of brinkmanship, but the boys held the aces: without them, there would be no new album, no more tours, no more Backstreet Boys; and no one wanted that. The boys had spent five years working towards getting to the top, but now they were there, the joy of success was being marred by rows and legal exchanges. It was a crazy, depressing scenario.

The legal wrangling continued into November and inevitably it fuelled rumours that the group was splitting up. In reality, there was never any serious talk of them going their separate ways, although they all agreed they wanted scope within their recording contract to do other work. Nick, for example, insisted on recording a duet with his brother Aaron and the other guys were determined to have self-penned solo contributions on the new album. In response to the question of splitting up, Nick replied: 'No way! I don't know where people are getting this idea from – we're the most successful we've ever been, and the happiest. We're ready for more.' Kevin added: 'We are five individuals and we have to allow each other to be himself as well as a group. Eventually there may come a time when we might want to take a break and each do our own thing for a while. When that time comes, we'll sit down as a group and decide what will happen.' Howie chipped in: 'We're in this for the long haul, even though some of us may move on to act or do solo records. But the Backstreet Boys will always be there. We'll do reunion tours like the Eagles and the Beach Boys, but we'll never

break up. Obviously we can't really predict what will happen to us in the future, but the fans have been great and we are thankful they are so dedicated. We want to keep going.'

Although the problems with the record company were not completely resolved, a breakthrough was finally reached and the guys were happy to fly to Sweden to begin laying down tracks for the third album and prepare ideas for the future. Many weeks' work had been lost because of the business wrangling and the schedule had been thrown into chaos, but at least now they could plan ahead with some certainty. It was decided that the new album would be released in the spring and would be followed by the biggest-ever Backstreet Boys world tour.

The Backstreet Boys brought 1998 to a quiet close by their standards. They were

so busy working on the album it left no time for promotion and at times the fans, who had been forced to contend with endless splitting-up stories, must have wondered what on earth had happened to their boys. This was reflected in the *Smash Hits* Awards in December when the guys had to be satisfied with one trophy for Best International Group, while Boyzone took all the main honours. Well, at least they had not been forgotten altogether, and besides, the Backstreet Boys knew things would be different the following year.

The guys packed their bags in Sweden and headed back to America to perform at the Billboard Music Awards in Las Vegas and to get in a few more days' recording in Florida. Then they had a blissful ten days off over Christmas to be with their families. Finally, the group ended 1998 in the best possible way, with a concert in Tampa and then a New Year's Eve show in Orlando. It had

been a turbulent year with many incredible highs and some terrible lows. The bitter financial problems had been hard to handle, but the boys had come through and were stronger and more united as a result of those tough experiences. They were now managing themselves and in complete control of their lives and they were even happy with their recording contracts. So, as they looked forward to 1999, the Backstreet Boys were filled with optimism and confidence, which was reflected in their fighting talk about the future. Kevin said: 'At first everyone had their set opinions of us, but you've got to prove yourself and they're starting to take us more seriously now. It's a lot of hard work, a lot of fun, very demanding, but I get a lot of satisfaction out of what I do. It's intense, it's crazy sometimes, but it is definitely exciting. We've got so much great stuff planned ahead. It's only going to get better.'

Brian added: 'I just want us to keep making good music for people of all ages to enjoy. We're not about a market or an image,

we're about good quality music. We believe that as long as we focus on the music and don't get distracted by other things, we'll hopefully be around for a long time.'

AJ was equally buoyant about the future. 'Everything's perfect for us now,' he enthused. 'We've got houses, cars, a bit of cash, our families and friends and this crazy, brilliant job.'

Meanwhile, Nick offered some advice to all would-be pop stars: 'If you want to succeed, just don't give up. That's how we got where we are today. We kept striving and working and never gave up. I've got just as equal a part in the band as the other four. That's what this group is all about – we decide on everything we do, from which record we're going to release, to what direction we're going in. We're all shareholders in our own company so everything is down to us.'

Howie added simply: 'Backstreet's Back and we're here for good. Thank you to all our fans for their support. Keep the Backstreet pride alive!'

Acknowledgements

I was lucky to have the kind help of many people while writing this book. I am very grateful to Scott Bennett and Nicole Peltz at Transcontinental Records in Florida for answering many queries and digging out information so swiftly. Many hard-working people have played an important role behind the scenes in helping the Backstreet Boys succeed over the years and three men – Robert Fischetti, Alan Siegel and Frank Sicoli – deserve a particular mention here. My special thanks goes to the irrepressible Lou Pearlman, the sixth Backstreet Boy and man with the plan, for his support with this book.

I am also grateful for the use of archive material from newspapers in America and articles from *Smash Hits* and *TV Hits* in the UK. At Boxtree, I would like to thank Adrian Sington and my editors, Clare Hulton and Verity Willcocks for their work on this project and my thanks also to my agent Jonathan Lloyd.

Finally, my best wishes go to the Backstreet Boys. They have worked tremendously hard since Day One and have proved to the doubters that they have the talent to deserve their pop star status. I appreciate that 1998 was an incredibly rewarding year for them, but also a testing one. I wish them fewer troubles in 1999 and continued success for the future.

Rob McGibbon, December 1998

Author

Rob McGibbon began his journalistic career in 1985 on the *Wimbledon News* in South London. He then worked as a news reporter and show-business writer on several national newspapers, before leaving to write books.

In 1990, he co-wrote the first biography of the New Kids on the Block with his father, Robin, also a journalist. They gambled on publishing the book themselves, before the band were famous in Britain, and it became a worldwide bestseller. In the next three years, they wrote biographies of England footballer Paul Gascoigne, TV presenter Phillip Schofield and Simply Red's lead singer Mick Hucknall.

Since then, Rob has written a biography of Take That, which was a bestseller in Germany, and four other pop music books published by Boxtree: *Boyzone on the Road*; *Boyzone, The True Story*; *Spice Power, The Inside Story* and *Backstreet Boys, Official Biography*. In between writing books, Rob is a freelance journalist and writes a range of celebrity interviews and features for national newspapers and magazines. He lives in London.